NOVA SCOTIA

JOURNEY ACROSS CANADA

Harry Beckett

The Rourke Book Co., Inc.
Vero Beach, Florida 32964

Harry Beckett M.A. (Cambridge), M.Ed. (Toronto), Dip.Ed. (Hull, England) has taught at the elementary and high school levels in England, Canada, France, and Germany. He has also travelled widely for a tour operator and a major book company.

Edited by Laura Edlund
Laura Edlund received her B.A. in English literature from the University of Toronto and studied Writing for Multimedia and Book Editing and Design at Centennial College. She has been an editor since 1986 and a traveller always.

ACKNOWLEDGMENTS
For photographs: Geovisuals (Kitchener, Ontario), The Canadian Tourism Commission and its photographers.
For reference: *The Canadian Encyclopedia, Encarta 1997, The Canadian Global Almanac, Symbols of Canada. Canadian Heritage*, Reproduced with the permission of the Minister of Public Works and Government Services Canada, 1997.
For maps: Promo-Grafx of Collingwood, Ont., Canada.

Library of Congress Cataloging-in-Publication Data

Beckett, Harry. 1936 -
   Nova Scotia / by Harry Beckett.
     p. cm. — (Journey across Canada)
   Includes index.
   Summary: An introduction to the geography, history, economy, major cities, and interesting sites of the eastern Canadian province that is almost completely surrounded by water.
   ISBN 1-55916-199-X (alk. paper)
   1. Nova Scotia—Juvenile literature.   [1. Nova Scotia.]
I. Title II. Series: Beckett, Harry, 1936 -   Journey across Canada.
F1037.4.B43 1997
917.16—dc21   97–6136
                                          CIP
                                          AC

Printed in the USA

TABLE OF CONTENTS

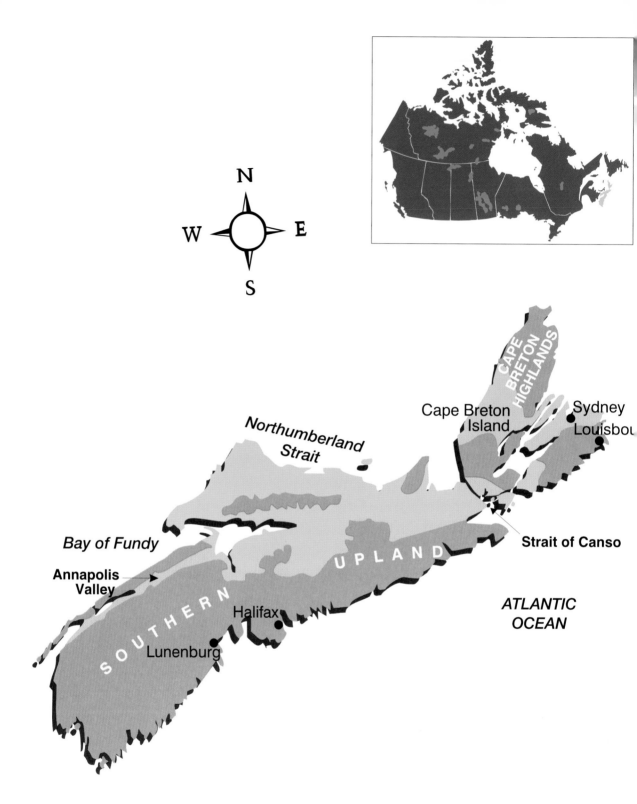

N

W   E

S

Cape Breton Island

CAPE BRETON HIGHLANDS

Sydney

Louisbou

Northumberland Strait

Bay of Fundy

Annapolis Valley

SOUTHERN   UPLAND

Strait of Canso

ATLANTIC OCEAN

Halifax

Lunenburg

PROVINCE OF NOVA SCOTIA

Chapter One

SIZE AND LOCATION

If you look at Nova Scotia, you may see the shape of a lobster, sticking out into the Atlantic Ocean. It is almost completely surrounded by water and is attached to its neighbour, New Brunswick, by a narrow neck of land. Between the coasts of the two provinces lies the Bay of Fundy. To the north, across the Northumberland Strait, lies Prince Edward Island.

Nova Scotia's northern part, Cape Breton Island, is separated from the rest of the province by the Strait of Canso. A **causeway** (KOZ way) helps people reach the island.

There are 3809 islands off the coast of Nova Scotia, including Sable Island, 193 kilometres (120 miles) out in the Atlantic Ocean.

Find out more...

- The total area of Nova Scotia is 55 490 square kilometres (21 426 square miles).
- The population is around 900 000.
- Sable Island is a long, sandy island known for wild horses and shipwrecks.

Chapter Two

GEOGRAPHY: LAND AND WATER

Nowhere in Nova Scotia is more than 80 kilometres (50 miles) from the sea. The coast, especially along the Atlantic Ocean, has many inlets that make excellent harbours.

The province is mostly rolling or rugged. The five separate regions of highland are separated by areas of lowland. A high ridge runs alongside

Peggy's Cove on one of the many rocky inlets

A ship left high and dry during low tide on the Bay of Fundy

the Bay of Fundy. Between it and the main Southern Upland lies the major lowland, the **fertile** (FUR tile) Annapolis Valley. Southern Cape Breton Island is flat, while the north is rugged and scenic. Coal is found under some of the lowlands.

The Bay of Fundy has the world's highest tides—up to 16 metres (52 feet). Except for the Annapolis River, Nova Scotia's rivers are short.

Chapter Three

WHAT IS THE WEATHER LIKE?

Nova Scotia gets most of its weather from the weather systems that cross the North American continent. However, the ocean helps cool down hot summers and warm up cold winters.

The cold Labrador Current, which flows down from the north, cools the winds and keeps the summers pleasantly mild. The spring comes late because these winds blow over the ice still floating offshore and cool the land.

In June and July, sea mists often form when the Labrador Current meets the warm, southern Gulf Stream. The fall is long and pleasant. The winters bring some snow, rain, and ice storms. Throughout the year, the climate is less mild away from the coast.

Find out more...

- Average daytime temperatures in Halifax range from 1.5°C (29° F) in January to 23.3°C (74° F) in July.
- Halifax has 170 days per year of wet weather.

Settlers coming ashore during a sea mist.

8

Chapter Four

MAKING A LIVING: HARVESTING THE LAND

Nova Scotia has a good climate for agriculture, but only a tenth of the land is farmed. Some farmland has been created by draining salt marshes.

The largest farming area is the Annapolis Valley, known for its apples. Another Nova Scotia fruit crop is wild blueberries. Seven out of ten farms are **livestock** (LIVE stok) farms. Most of these keep dairy cows.

Three quarters of Nova Scotia is forested. The pulp and paper industry uses most of the wood, but your Christmas tree may come from here.

Nova Scotia's fishing industry is the largest in Atlantic Canada. The fish are sold fresh, frozen, dried, or salted. Nova Scotia lobster and scallops are famous.

If a lobster is too small, it must be returned to the sea.

Find out more...

- Another important lowland area lies along the Northumberland Strait.
- Atlantic fish stocks are getting smaller and smaller.

The **Micmac** (MIK mak) peoples were in Nova Scotia long before the French named it Acadia. Control of the region passed from France to Britain and back several times before Britain seized Fort Louisbourg in 1758.

Settlers came in waves from France, Britain, and Germany. Twenty thousand **Loyalists** (LOY uh lists)

A military display at Halifax Citadel can be noisy.

A day in the life of Fort Louisbourg

came to Nova Scotia during the American
Revolution (1775-83). Some were Black slaves
looking for freedom. In 1755, Britain forced the
French population to leave.

Later, in the nineteenth century, jobs in the
coal fields brought settlers from Europe.

Chapter Six

MAKING A LIVING: FROM INDUSTRY

Three quarters of Nova Scotia's electricity comes from generators powered by local coal. The rest comes from power from the tides or hydro-electricity.

Most manufacturers are small and use the resources of the province. They make paper from pulp wood, preserve vegetables and fruit, and prepare fish for sale.

Halifax, on the main Atlantic sea routes, is Canada's third largest container port. Ferries run from Nova Scotia to Maine, New Brunswick, Newfoundland, and Prince Edward Island.

Nova Scotia draws tourists with fine beaches and more historic sites than any other province, except Québec.

Find out more...

- Oil and natural gas have been found off Sable Island and the southern coast.
- Service industries (tourism, transportation, government, etc.) employ three quarters of all of Nova Scotia.

A dock in Halifax, with containers that can be moved by ship, train, or truck

Chapter Seven

IF YOU GO THERE...

Fort Louisbourg might be your first destination. Parts of its **fortifications** (for tih fih KAY shunz), its **citadel** (SIT uh del), **quay** (kee), and old town have been rebuilt.

Over one million visitors a year go to Nova Scotia. Many visit Fort Anne, in Annapolis Royal, the oldest fort in Nova Scotia. And crowds go to the fishing village of Peggy's Cove, with its famous lighthouse. In Halifax, the Halifax Citadel and Historic Properties are popular spots.

The Bluenose, a champion **schooner** (SKOO nur) was built in Lunenburg, and the Bluenose II, an exact copy, can be seen sailing in Nova Scotia's waters. Fine beaches and pleasant weather make Nova Scotia Canada's "ocean playground."

The Bluenose II *under full sail*

Find out more...

• The Bluenose can also be seen on the Canadian dime.

• Lunenburg is a town on the Atlantic coast, settled largely by Germans.

Chapter Eight

MAJOR CITIES

Halifax, Nova Scotia's capital, is the most important centre in the Maritimes. Trade with Europe and the West Indies helped it to grow. Now, most people work at military bases, at container ports, or in public service. Halifax has four universities and an international airport.

In 1749, 2500 settlers came to found the city. A thousand of them died during their first winter.

The city of Halifax with its port and, in the background, the fortifications

The Historic Properties in downtown Halifax

Halifax has an important military history. During World War I (1914-18) arms and troops left from there for Europe. In 1917, much of the city was destroyed and 1600 people were killed when a ship exploded in the harbour.

Sydney, the main city on Cape Breton Island, stands on rich coal fields and is a steel-making centre. Ferries to Newfoundland leave from nearby North Sydney.

Chapter Nine

SIGNS AND SYMBOLS

Nova Scotia is Latin for "New Scotland." The province's symbols reflect its Scottish history.

The coat of arms bears the Scottish Cross of Saint Andrew. The colours are reversed in order to distinguish Nova Scotia's arms from Scotland's. On the cross is the Scottish coat of arms. Above the shield are the Scottish thistle, the hand of protection, and the laurel leaf of peace, triumph, and conquest. The unicorn is also a Scottish symbol, and the warrior represents the Native peoples.

The flag is the Scottish coat of arms on a reversed Saint Andrew's cross.

The Latin motto means "One defends and the other conquers."

Nova Scotia's flower is the mayflower.

Nova Scotia's flag, coat of arms, and flower

GLOSSARY

causeway (KOZ way) — a raised roadway between wet ground or shallow water

citadel (SIT uh del) — a fortress protecting a town

fertile (FUR tile) — rich, good for growing things in

fortification (for tih fih KAY shun) — a place that is strengthened against attack

livestock (LIVE stok) — farm animals

Loyalist (LOY uh list) — the people of American colonies who sided with Britain in the American Revolution

Micmac (MIK mak) — a Native people of eastern Canada

quay (kee) — a solid landing place for ships to load and unload

schooner (SKOO nur) — a ship with two or more masts and sails

Scottish dancing at one of Nova Scotia's many festivals

INDEX